THE

FITNESS OF THE PRIVATE SCHOOL

TO

British Wants & the British Character.

A PAPER READ BEFORE THE ASSOCIATION
OF PRIVATE SCHOOLMASTERS.

BY

THOMAS WYLES, F.G.S., F.R.His.S., M.C.P.

Coventry :

CURTIS & BEAMISH, HERTFORD STREET.

—

1886.

THE FITNESS OF THE PRIVATE SCHOOL

TO

BRITISH WANTS and the BRITISH CHARACTER.

A PAPER READ BEFORE THE ASSOCIATION OF PRIVATE SCHOOLMASTERS, BY

THOMAS WYLES, F.G.S., F.R.His.S., M.C.P.

Descent. Our modern education, as our modern civilization, is the outcome of past times—the legacy of our forefathers. We look back upon the dark ages when Rome wrapped her mantle of ignorance and superstition around us, and decreed a civilization without letters, and without the culture which letters alone can bring. These were times when kingly courtesy, a rude chivalry, and the pride of birth were the highest civilizing aspirations; when unrestrained passion and fierce conflict marked our social and our national life.

But the Divine purpose does not stop. The wet blanket of Rome's oppressive influence yielded to the inherent forces of our spiritual life. The conspiracy of priest and baron—those mediæval types of spiritual death and oppressive degradation—was in its later days shaken by the volcanic outbursts of a new and spiritual life. Wycliffe, Huss Jerome, Savanarola, stand out of these dark ages like the dead volcanoes of a past geological period, and the streams of spiritual truth which flowed from their inspirations lay deep down in the souls of men, diffusing its fertilizing power, and supplying an undergrowth of spiritual forces, which were ready at the revival of letters to spring up and grow into our marvellous modern civilization.

Inheritance. Modern education is our inheritance from the revival of letters. Modern languages were then in process of development, and had no grammar—the science of language. There had been almost no scientific investigation, and empiricism passed for science. Art was left to the inspiration of the few, and was mainly subservient to religious zeal and priestly purposes. Logic and metaphysics supplied the data for the puerile wranglings of the schoolmen. The Latin language and literature—to which later on Greek was added—seemed the only means of literary culture. It is not my function here to discuss the wisdom or unwisdom of adhering so much as we do to this means of education; but I may note that since the revival of letters there has been no such stagnation of intellectual growth as in mediæval times; that at first slowly, but with accelerating force, light has streamed in upon us; that every accession to human knowledge and human thought has been an addition to our expansive power; that in this century especially, discoveries in science, and moral, intellectual and material development, have been a marvel hard for younger men to realize; and that surely we may find in all this some educational means better than the dry crusts of Greek and Latin—some culture in modern languages and their valuable literature—some "sweetness and light" in the study of knowledge itself, as well as in the study of the tools of knowledge.

Nearly all our endowments date from Tudor times. After then—was not the education of youth provided for—at least so far as they needed education? And why should men further trouble about it? Private schools there were—Milton had one, probably the type of many others. Great impetus was given to private schools by the Acts of Uniformity, especially that of 1662, when the 2,000 Nonconforming clergy were largely driven to engage in education for bread, and by virtue of their nonconformity, were disqualified for employment in the endowed schools. Henceforth these two distinctive forms of education were operative in our country. The private school complementary to the endowed school.

We have not forgotten our school days, nor schools as they too often were in the first half of this century. It was a rare thing, then, to find any rule in a boys' school but that of the stick; any appeal but to fear. Moral forces were rarely comprehended or believed in. We have a shuddering recollection of seeing boys caned and birched for mental defects for which they were not responsible, and which the master was at once incapable of recognizing or remedying. There was little discipline but that of the martinet. It was consistent that a rule, which took so little cognizance of the rational and the moral, should be linked with narrowest views of intellectual learning. Master and pupil stood in a false position to each other. The pupil was subjected to unreasoning obedience; the tutor assumed an authority which was arbitrary and unjust, and too often enforced obedience by unmanly and brutal chastisement. The relation was severely autocratic, and often repellant rather than attractive. Such influences were not unfrequently the germs whence grew the tyranny and vice which followed school. If men grew self-governed and virtuous, they did so mainly by subjective worth, or domestic, moral, and religious forces.

Milton, Lock, Cowper, Dymond, Channing, Simpson, and a cloud of witnesses at different times indicated the defects of our educational practice, and pointed to better things. But their monitions fell on soils rendered sterile by the prejudice, conservatism, and vested interests embodied in our endowed schools, and too often copied in our private schools. Here and there, perhaps, kindred souls offered a fertile soil to the living truths sown by such writers for the better education of British youth. Gradually these truths are taking possession of the public mind. They are chiefly active in the minds of our producing and mercantile classes, and these are the classes who have been almost wholly educated in our private schools.

Modern Conditions. From various causes, but mainly from the marked characteristics of our national spirit of independence, the private school has been a chief factor in the education of Englishmen. Side by side with the endowed school, and more sensitive than that to national wants, it has been very largely supported.

Of late the tendency of many writers on educational matters is to ignore or depreciate the private school. We propose, therefore, in this paper to discuss the question, which of these two kinds of institutions—the public school, or the private school, is the better conditioned to adapt itself to the progressive thought, and knowledge, and social and material development of successive generations ; to fit in its educational activities with the wheels of time ? By virtue of its endowment, and its chartered purposes ; by virtue of its concrete embodiment of the then limited lines of thought ; by virtue of the conservatism which besets all endowments, and the paralysis which attends them ; it may be assumed that the endowed school would be unlikely to lead in educational progress. Whatever the limitations of thought attending the earlier institutions of private schools, these, dependent as they are on the supply of felt wants, have been more ready to recognize these wants, and to follow the light and leading of our progressive intellectual life.

The fitness of existing institutions must be estimated by a survey of what has gone before. The fitness of what is must be tested by the place it takes in the progress of the world. Up to the first half of this century our education was characterized by the saddest misunderstanding or disregard of its means, purposes, or power. No part of the educational field was free from the influence of this general misapprehension. The low conception of the teacher which prevailed was largely responsible for his defects. Men as well as boys have a marked tendency to be what they are thought to be. And here the endowed schoolmaster had a very decided advantage. He owed his position to a public or quasi-public appointment. He at least could claim the prestige of a public office. If it was the duty of any school master to exalt his office, raise the standard of his work, appeal to and cultivate a higher public want in education; this was surely the function of the endowed schoolmaster. He could feel and plead independence of public caprice or ignorance, and manifest the dignity of his office. Did he do this?

Progress. For the last half century there has been a growing fermentation on the subject of education. Government has taken in hand the schools for the mass; the Royal College of Preceptors has done much to raise the status of the teacher, to broaden the means of education, and to improve the methods in our secondary schools; and, thanks to Mr. Acland and Dr. Temple, the Universities are holding out a friendly hand to our schools, saying, " we will see what you are doing, and testify of your work." Under these auspices education has, during thirty years past, made rapid strides. A wider range of subjects is being introduced; better methods of teaching are being adopted; a more just apprehension of the relation between teacher and pupil prevails; and the interaction of mental, moral, and physical education is better understood. And who have been most susceptible of these enlightening influences—most ready to give them practical effect? Mr. Brice, by no means a friendly witness, tells us that " the private schools have done what the endowed schools have neglected, and have by their competition greatly raised the tone of the endowed schools."

Endowments Coincidently with all this there has been an in-
versus creasing demand for broader knowledge and higher
Freedom. moral qualifications in the schoolmaster. It is beginning to be seen that he who undertakes the high office of youthful training, should himself understand the mental, moral, and physical constitution of youth. He can scarcely educate— using that term literally—who knows not what he is to educate. A right apprehension of man's mental and moral being is essential to the effective exercise of his faculties for mental and moral training. Unhappily it is not every teacher who has grasped the subject of education in its highest and most important bearings : who has made the education of youth a philosophical study. But it may be asserted that there are among our private schoolmasters men of high culture and intelligence; men profoundly inspired with the love of youth; men with " the energy, facility of illustration, flow of spirits, self-control, and a touch of enthusiasm," without which Mr. Fearon says, " a man can never become a good schoolmaster." Whether in all this the private schoolmaster compares favourably with the endowed, let the Commission of 1869 upon our endowed schools reply. The first 280 pp. of that Report abound with repeated and often severe complaint of incompetence, ignorance of the art of teaching, waste of time and

...ngth by bad methods, and unproductive work in the endowed schools. And again, they say :—

"The perpetual sense of responsibility to the parents, which is necessarily felt by the master of a private school, is not without its advantages. The master has the strongest pressure of pecuniary interest to keep him to his duty; the result is, that he is more often exact and careful in minute details. The particulars required by the parents are tolerably certain to be well done. If parental interference be irksome, yet it is stimulating; and in all probability it very rarely happens that a master of a private school sinks into carelessness or neglect of duty; for if he does. his school soon quits him. The scandalous cases, of which there are too many, of masters retaining endowed schools with few, or even without any scholars, show how far utter neglect of duty may go, when a man's interest in no way depends on the discharge of his duty. Before a grammar schoolmaster thus emptied his school, he must as a general rule have been regardless of the obligations of his office for years. Many scholars must have suffered from his neglect before it was found out. Had he been a private schoolmaster, the first withdrawal on account of neglect would have been a sharp warning, and he would have been spurred to double effort to prevent a second. The master of an endowed school has often been able to fall asleep; the master of a private school cannot."

All this is the effect of the endowment. Endowed schoolmasters are not morally inferior to others. Remembering that they are drawn largely—almost wholly—from university life, and are, assumedly, men of high culture, they ought to be men of high moral type. No, it is not the men that are worse, but it is the endowment, the absence of ever pressing necessity, and our instinctive love of ease, which tend to demoralize. None of us can say that he would be what he is, were he to transfer his energies to an endowed school.

The waves of human progress roll on with accelerated force, and he best rides their crests who is most sensitive to their influence. The private schoolmaster has ever been in closest sympathy with the social life of our people. He has had almost no professional status, no prestige, no endowment, and happily no "corporate or statutory control." The goodness or badness of his school has been a co-ordinate of the public will. He exists only as he ministers to a public want. Subject to the keenest influences of competition, he must move with the times; and the tendency of the most earnest and energetic schoolmasters is to move in advance of the times. He is forced to catch the spirit of improvement, and to shape his principles and methods to the public wants. The Commissioners themselves bear testimony to the more impressive influence of private teaching. They say :—

"The private schoolmasters are the men who most often make improvements, and discover new methods. The private school offers a field for their experiments, which the public school can hardly do."

And they further quote Mr. Fitch, who says :—

"Among the private schoolmasters are some who evince an enthusiasm in the work of teaching, a knowledge of the best methods, and a wealth of educational expedients, which are quite remarkable. They have teaching the business of their lives, and have devoted to it enorm labour and thought."

May we not predict that it will be an evil day in the life of this country, should the private school disappear, or fail to exercise its stimulating force upon the education and independent character of our countrymen ?

Reorganization :— Will it counteract the tendency of endowments ? Since 1869, under the penetrating influence of the Endowed Schools Commissioners, the educational endowments, and to some extent the non-educational, have been thrown into their crucible, and recast in greatly improved institutions all over the country. These remodelled schools are on a broader basis ; have more or less enlarged their course of study, and improved their methods ; have generally large and well-arranged new buildings ; and in every way appeal with greatly enhanced force to the wants of the community.

Yet they have retained a large measure of their ancient conservatism, and although they have more flexibility than formerly, they cannot adapt themselves so readily to progressive public wants, as can the private school. One feature especially gives them an enhanced competitive power with the private school : the endowment is more or less subordinated to the payments of the pupils ; to this extent they contain the element of free trade, which tends to counteract the stagnation and decay inherent in all endowments ; and to this extent they assume the more active vitality of private institutions.

Still the paralysing element of endowment is there, and Lord Sherbrook says :—

"It is the nature and essence of endowments to injure education, by putting to sleep the diligence of teachers—by bribing parents to accept teaching at a cheaper rate, regardless of its character—by discouraging healthy private enterprise—and by fostering an undue adherence to obsolete subjects and methods of instruction. The one thing that can always be said for an endowment is that in its inception it is sure to be popular. There is money to spend—there are buildings to erect—there is patronage—there is power—above all, there is novelty. But what is the result ? The period of excitement is succeeded by a period of languor, and the process of degeneration begins slowly and insidiously, but surely, to relax the sinews of exertion and enterprise."

Again Lord Sherbrook says :—

"From first to last the Commissioners assume that the ordinary principles of political economy are inapplicable to education ; that Britons are not to be trusted with the education of their children ; that the State can best determine what education should be ; and they use the endowments to bribe them to accept the education which they provide. They assume the possibility that the zeal and devotion of private enterprise and private responsibility can be infused into councils and boards of governors."

Whether, and to what extent, they will demonstrate this possibility must be left to the future, but we may not forget that law is immutable, its operations constant, its effects certain. A French writer (Turgot) says :—

"Endowments, whatever be their apparent utility, carry in themselves an irremediable vice which they derive from their very nature—the impossibility of maintaining the execution of their purpose; zeal will not communicate itself from age to age. There is no incorporation which does not at least lose the spirit of its origin, endowments will presumably become one day useless, perhaps injurious, and will be so for a long time."

Adam Smith asks the following pertinent questions :—

"Have endowments contributed to private education? Have they encouraged the diligence and improved the abilities of teachers? Have they directed education to useful objects and to public wants? Or has not education in its freer moods and more natural courses, more readily adapted itself to progressive development?"

And in answer he declares

"That the exertion of most men is governed by the necessity for making it; that the endowments of schools and colleges have necessarily diminished more or less the necessity of application in the teachers; that energy and application co-ordinate with the reward their exercise brings; that when, as in some colleges and schools, the endowment supplies the whole salary, interest and the love of ease are set in direct opposition to duty; and that to the extent that endowments attract pupils independent of the merit and reputation of the teachers, the necessity of merit and reputation is lessened."

Lord Sherbrook further says :—

"Few people will seriously argue that a teacher whose pupils are induced to come to him by pecuniary advantages held out to their parents, and whose income is more or less independent of his success, will be as energetic or as successful as one possessing neither of these advantages."

Greater fitness of the Private School. The Commissioners themselves say that

"It is in private schools rather than in public that we are to look for improvements, and the discovery of new methods."

That is, in private schools there is progress, there is the power of adaptation to new circumstances. All the claims set up for endowed schools under public control, imply that British parents are unfit or unable to judge of what is good for the education of their children; that they have less discernment as to what is good and profitable in this all important function, than have the governors of endowments under State control. And yet at this day, and still more when these Commissioners issued their **Report,**

"In our great universities very little is learned from the professors who have fixed salaries; somewhat more from tutors who have some interest, pecuniary and personal, in the success of their colleges; but the main weight of teaching, especially for the highest honours, rests on private tutors or coaches, who have no endowment—no university status—but who work under the stimulus of need and competition. They, with everything against them, are the real moving spirits of our universities.

They form the mind of youth ; they regulate indirectly the tendencies of thought ; and without notoriety, without recognition, without public responsibility, do the work, while the rich endowments are divided among those who do it not."

The Commissioners further say in their Report :—

"Public schools are too indulgent to idleness, and consequently send out a large proportion of men of idle habits, and empty and uncultivated minds."

Professor Price says :—

"The young men from our public schools are far worse prepared as to their mathematical attainments than those from other schools. . . . Through the Oxford Local Examinations we learn that the standard of knowledge for mathematical subjects, both for extent and accuracy, of boys belonging to middle class schools, is far superior to that of candidates for matriculation from public schools."

Mr. Gladstone says :—

"The value of the work we get out of the mass of boys from our public schools is scandalously small."

Canon Farrar says that

"The classical education of the public schools as it is carried out is a deplorable failure . . . . a gigantic negation."

Dr. Whewell quotes a Chancellor's Medalist, who speaks of

"The total absence in the university examination of any scientific and well-grounded knowledge on any classical subject whatever. What is required is not knowledge, but skill."

Like utterances from the Public Schools Commission Report and other sources could be added without limit. These will go far to show that past experiences closely accord with the laws of political economy by demonstrating that our efforts to set them aside in education as in other matters result in deplorable failure, and that British parents who elect the education of the private school for their sons, do not so very much err in judgment. The testimony of the Commissioners themselves may be quoted in support of this allegation. In the closing pages of their Report they are constrained to say,

"That many of the private schools are doing very good work ; that they have a great advantage over the endowed schools in their greater elasticity ; that they can more readily adapt themselves to the needs of the day ; that they are not hampered by rules ; that the master of a private school can make changes at will, and supply that which is needed."

Commenting on this, Lord Sherbrook says :—

"I should rather say they are peculiarly useful in an age which some consider as one of vast progress, and all must admit to be one of violent and rapid transition ; they possess an element of popularity, and of fitness for these rapid changes, which more deeply rooted and established institutions cannot pretend to ; and though from their very nature they are incapable of being organized and incorporated into a cast-iron system, they are, on that very account, only the more fit for supporting the chief burden of educating the middle classes."

Educational wants vary. The educational wants of a country so diverse in its employments as ours, are by no means uniform. The private schools are peculiarly adapted to meet these diversified wants by virtue of their freedom and flexibility. In point of fact, they have supplied these varied wants, and hence their varied character. The Commissioners say :—

"The needs of the different parts of England are so different that a uniform reorganization of the schools of the country is neither possible nor expedient, that the character of the population must be considered ; and the kind of education to which the people have been already accustomed should have its proper weight."

Now, "the kind of education to which the people have been accustomed" had been given in private schools ; and it is some satisfaction to find the Commissioners thus compelled to recognize its worth. They say :—

"It is plain that many private schools are doing very good work."

We are told by Mr. Fitch that

"Almost all the educational enterprise of the last few years has originated with private teachers."

And the Commissioners tell us that the

"Grammar schools are likely to be in the rear of improvements, unless some means can be devised for keeping them much more alert than they have hitherto been."

The necessity of increased vigilance is clearly seen by the Commissioners, for they say

"The [endowed] schools are almost always less useful than they might be, often useless, sometimes mischievous ; chiefly because they do not teach what is wanted. They need to have their work precisely defined, and then to be kept to that work."

Conscious as the Commissioners must be that it is to the apathy and inadequacy of governing bodies, and the depressing influence of endowments, must be attributed the failure of the endowed schools ; they yet think it safer and better to leave the ordering of the work of education to governing bodies, than to parents who are so closely related to, and so greatly interested in the education of their children, and it is remarkable that in the recasting of our endowed schools no provision is made by inspection or otherwise for the maintenance of the integrity of their work.

The Commissioners evidently look for some amendment of constitution and character in an elected board of governors as against a co-optative board of trustees ; and it is probable that for a time these more broadly appointed boards may bring light and energy to bear upon their work, as indeed they are doing at the present time ; but ultimately the commercial principle, if it have a fair field, is bound to prove by virtue of the laws that control it, the better adapted to the varied wants of a community so intimately affected by commercial considerations as the British people.

How Schoolmasters are made. Public schoolmasters, both head and subordinate, receive their appointments almost wholly upon the qualification of a university education. It is an acknowledged mistake to suppose that scholarship and clerical office necessarily make a schoolmaster. Teaching is an art to be acquired by specific training, and public schoolmasters have declared that they learned to be teachers by processes at once painful to themselves and injurious to their pupils. The long continued failure of many of our public schoolmasters is due to the fact that obtaining their appointments directly from college fellowships, and without practical knowledge of school life and work, they have often been unable to develop that loving sympathy with boys, or the keen moral discernment which must underlie and intertwine themselves with all really successful school work. Dr. Donaldson says :—

"The teachers in the public schools of England are commonly highly educated men, yet the Commissioners tell us that taken as a whole their teaching has been a miserable failure. Why? Because most of them do not know how to teach. They employ methods which violate every law of psychology, and persist in practices which are injurious to the human mind."

The better private schools are now mainly directed by university graduates or men of high scholarship, who have passed through the ordeal of long training as assistant masters. Not a few have transferred their energies from the public to the private school, because the latter offers greater scope to their felt power in education. There is an increasing demand in private schools for assistants whose scholarship has been tested by university examination, provided they have proved their skill in teaching, and their moral and disciplinary power by adequate experience. Inexperienced assistants commonly offer only for subordinate positions, and if in their early career they show unfitness in scholarship, teaching power, temperament, or character, they are pretty sure to be weeded out, and have to take their abilities to other than the educational market. A large proportion of the men now offering for assistant masters in private schools are strong and worthy men—sound scholars—apt and effective teachers—sympathetic in their relations to boys—conscientious in the performance of duty. Non-university men commonly begin teaching when young, and by varied experiences in smaller schools with the aid and direction of the principal, acquire considerable experience and skill before they can get an appointment in a higher school. In well-reputed private schools no tutor can hold a place unless his scholarship be sufficient, his teaching effective, and his discipline and influence good. And this is the training from which with few exceptions our head masters spring. As a rule the men who will to take the sole charge of a private school, are men with more than ordinary energy; men who feel their power—are actuated by high principle—experienced in their work—and cognizant of the severe toil and heavy responsibility which attend the life of a private schoolmaster. Such are the men; and the Commissioners bear frequent testimony to their energy, skill, and devotion to their work.

The importance of sole control and responsibility. Again, the head master of a public school is not only fettered by limited control over his subordinates, but by corporation statutes, testamentary charges, the regulation of trustees and governing bodies; and very grave difficulties in government have arisen from this limited authority. In a private school the control of the head masters is absolute, and it is not possible that the harmony of the school can be long disturbed, or the mental and moral work seriously affected by differences between the head and assistant masters. Mr. Brice tells us that

"The school succeeds best wherein there is no divided responsibility."

And Mr. Stanton, in his report, says

"An able and intelligent private schoolmaster has a scope and freedom which no master of an endowed or proprietary school can enjoy. He has no corporate or statutory control. To an able man this is an advantage, and all our greatest schoolmasters have been those who have been least interfered with."

Varied talents: individual care. The bulk of boys as of men lies within the average. The extremes of the gifted and the feeble are few. The gifted want simply direction, and will educate themselves with little trouble to the teachers. The average want more help, especially as they shade down towards the feeble. The feeble require much help, and gentle care and encouragement. A private schoolmaster has a direct interest in making the best out of every boy. In the smaller classes of a well-ordered private school, these feeble boys are specially provided for, and call forth and receive the highest talent of the master. In the large classes of our public schools they are often sadly neglected, sometimes wholly overlooked; and not a few after spending years in a public school are finally transferred to a private one, with the hope, more or less realized, that their neglected powers may be galvanized into some activity.

Oversight, and moral responsibility. "Mother," said an Eton boy, lately, "don't come to see me unless you come swell, it won't do me any good with the boys." This simple fact reveals the pestilent pride of these boys—not the pride of worth, but the hateful pride of pomp, and place, and wealth. Nor may we shut our eyes to the occasional rents in the curtain which reveal graver faults, such as questionable morals, social tyranny and brutality, serious breaches of discipline, wild destruction of property. A private schoolmaster would be ruined by events which occur in public schools and attract but little note. He dare not allow even the semblance of the coarse brutality revealed by a late event in King's College School. His interests compel a strict regard for the moral and social life of his school. He must vigilantly guard against vice and coarseness; protect the weak, and teach the strong that truest manliness lies in a chivalrous defence of the feeble. We do not hesitate to say that, taking the mass of the better private schools, they will in all matters of conduct compare most favourably with our public schools.

Buildings. Nor may we lose sight of the question of buildings. In past times little regard was given to these, and they were often bad for both public and private schools. But long before the Schools Enquiry Commission of 1868, many of our private schools were conducted in large and suitable buildings, amply supplied with educational material. At the present time a private school with indifferent premises has small chance. Large capital expenditure in building is an important factor in the success of a school.

Private Schools must be. The Commissioners realize the fact that private schools must be, and they say that

" By their competition they have greatly raised the tone of the endowed schools; that this competition will always be of great value; that the best system risks the loss of energy, if undisturbed by rivalry; and that it is hoped the endowed schools will not again be allowed to slip into the condition which has in so many places transferred the majority of boys to private schools."

This is complimentary to the laws of political economy and to private schools.

How have our business men been educated? Scarcely do you find a trace in the Commissioners' Report of any reference to our vast mercantile community, the glory of our country, and the very core of its progress and prosperity. The spending classes, which are mainly educated in our public schools, seem to be chiefly in their view. The earning classes are largely ignored. Yet our national progress, and our national wealth, have at all events grown to be what they are very largely under the education given in private schools. Our productive and trading classes of all grades have effected the vast national development which is the glory and pride of Britons, with the knowledge and culture obtained almost wholly in private schools. One of the most estimable of our poets has taunted our great middle classes with " Philistinism " (whatever that may mean), and a lack of " sweetness and light." Faults we have, and we may feel grateful to those who tell us of them. The moralist may mourn over our national ignorance, our national sins, our national crimes, and the idleness which generates selfishness :—But he turns the shield, and he rejoices over a philanthropy which is as broad as the world ; a religious zeal which is ever struggling to lift the fallen and degraded ; a deep sympathy with suffering which is striving in a thousand ways to soothe and to alleviate; the "light" of a divine life, and the "sweetness" of human sympathies, not paralleled. Where would be the wealth and power, the moral worth and influence of our country if this great middle class element was eliminated? What was Britain when she had no middle class? The growth of our middle class has been contemporary with the growth of our wealth and power, and progressive with freer religious activities, and the independence of the private school. It may well be held the pride of the private school that its educational work has ministered so largely and so well to the social life of our great middle class, to the development and moral worth of this vast mercantile community.

In the past the greatest enterprise and the most successful progress in education have lain with the private schools; and, impelled by a keener competition; watched by a more enlightened and vigilant public; governed by higher intellectual and moral purposes; these schools may appeal with increasing force to our countrymen.

The School-master. The man who is a true schoolmaster; whose soul is garnished with a halo of divine love; who brings to bear upon his responsible duties an exalted desire to do good; whose genius prompts him to be ever seeking for higher principles and better methods; who believes that even the best teacher has something yet to learn; such a man finds in a private school the best of fields; because there he is untrammelled by limiting conditions; free from the influence of many masters; can catch the fire of human progress, and apply it to the material which he has to work upon; is sensitive to the touch of parental care; and alive to the semi-parental responsibilities of his office. The Commissioners acknowledge this; and it is a matter of educational history that all, or nearly all, educational reformers have sprung from this large and productive field of educational labour.

The Report of the Commissioners is drawn up with a marked bias in favour of public schools. We have thought well, therefore, to draw largely upon that Report, as of more than ordinary value and importance.